Slow down, Little Junie

Written by
Kalee Boisvert
Illustrated by
Ponyo Nguyen

There once was a little girl named Junie who ran everywhere.

She ran to say hi to her fish in the morning.

She ran in circles around the kitchen table, trying to decide which chair felt right that day.

She ran away to hide when it was bath time.

And she even ran in her dreams.

"I just have so much to do!" she'd giggle,
hair flying behind her like a kite.
The world was full of exciting things,
and Junie didn't want to miss a single one.

One time, as Junie was running ahead, she heard her mom call from behind, "Slow down, little Junie. You just missed a blue butterfly landing on the tree."

Junie stopped,
just for a second
and looked.
But the butterfly was already gone

Another time, her mom said,
"Slow down, little Junie, or you'll miss the sound of the wind whispering to the flowers."

Then there was the time her mom gently said, "Slow down, little Junie, or you won't hear your own feet say thank you to the Earth."

But today, Junie was off again
zooming through the yard like a race car,
going so fast nobody could catch her.

She jumped over sidewalk cracks like they were lava and sang the kind of songs that just popped into her head.

She had so much to do today.
She didn't want to stop.
Not when the fun was still going.

But then, just before the sky began to fade, they were in their backyard when her mom reached for her hand and said, "Let's stop to watch this magical sunset."

Junie grumbled, just a little.
She had been right in the middle
of lining up all her toy cars by color.
She hadn't been planning to stop.

But when she looked up,
the sky had turned orange and pink and gold
just like the finger painting on the fridge.
The one where Junie had mushed all the brightest colors
together because it felt happy.

Everything was quiet but it actually felt okay.
Not like the boring quiet where a grown-up says "shhh,"
but the kind of quiet that felt like
something special might happen.

And Junie felt it too, right there on her arms,
like the sunset was brushing her with warm paint.
Junie was glad she hadn't missed it.
And maybe—just maybe—this time,
Mom was right about stopping.

That evening, her mom finally caught her
and wrapped her up in a hug
and a bunch of bedtime tickles.

Junie giggled and wiggled, but let herself be steered toward her room. Pajamas on. Teeth brushed. She climbed under the covers and snuggled into her cozy bed.

Her mom sat at the edge of her bed,
smiling like she had a secret to tell.

"You're like a shooting star," she said.
"Bright, fast, and magical.
But stars don't see where they're
going when they fly so fast."

Junie scrunched up her nose.
"But I don't want to miss anything."

Her mom nodded gently.
"Sometimes, when you slow down…
You see more.
You hear more.
You feel more.
You find things your heart has been quietly trying to show you."

The next morning,
Junie tried something new.
She walked,
Just to be a little bit slower.

The breeze greeted her,
like it had been waiting
for her to finally notice it.
It caught bits of her hair,
tickling her cheeks like it was
playing a quiet game of tag.

And then she stopped.
On a tree branch, a blue butterfly.
Its wings opened and closed, slow as a breath, like it wasn't in a rush either.
It stayed. Just long enough.
And Junie stayed too.

After that, she didn't always go fast.
She ran when she wanted to feel wild.
She walked when she wanted to see.

And she stood still when
she didn't want to miss the secrets.

And now Junie spotted magic everywhere, tiny treasures she found on her own and loved surprising her mom with.

www.ingramcontent.com/pod-product-compliance
Lightning Source LLC
LaVergne TN
LVHW070225110826
845147LV00003B/644
* 9 7 8 1 0 6 9 6 4 9 5 8 4 *